Contents

What you need

Do you like dragons?
Here's how to make
a dragon card.

These are the things you will need:

Some stiff, coloured card

An old envelope

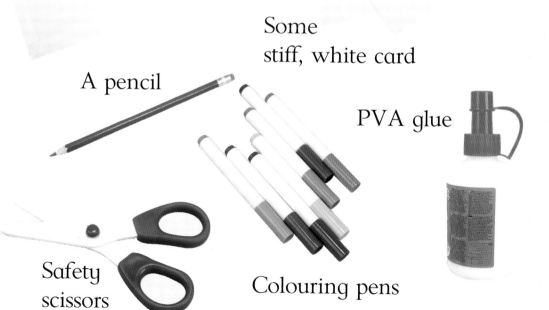

Some stiff, white card

A pencil

PVA glue

Safety scissors

Colouring pens

5

Cutting out the snout

First, draw this shape on the envelope corner. Make it about 10cm along each side.

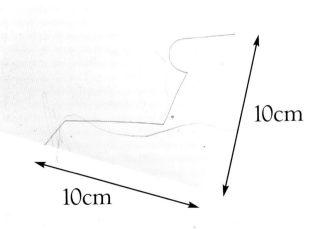

10cm

10cm

Cut out
the shape.

This will be the
snout of the
dragon.

7

Colouring the snout

Draw on some nostrils and oval shapes.

Then colour in the top of the snout.

8

You can colour in the mouth, too.

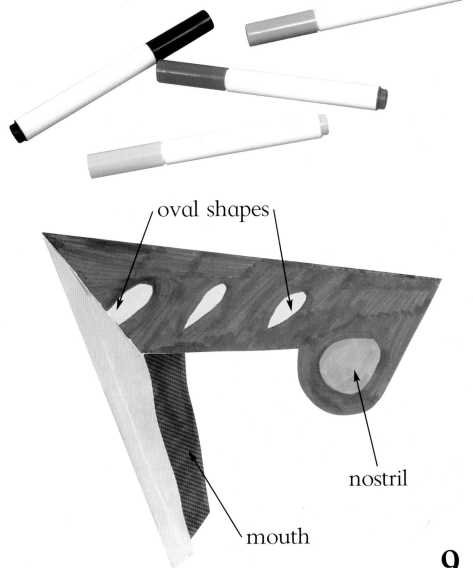

oval shapes

nostril

mouth

Drawing the dragon

Fold the piece of stiff card in half.

Flatten down the fold.

10

Draw a dragon's face across the inside of the card.

You could add a tail, too.

Colouring the dragon

Next, use the pens to colour in your dragon.

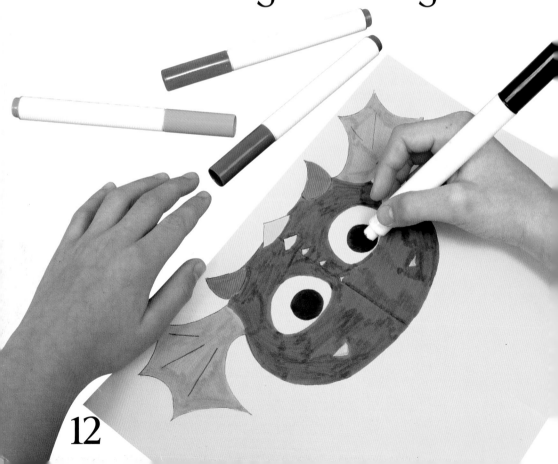

13

Gluing the snout

Glue the sides of the bottom part of the snout across the inside of the fold.

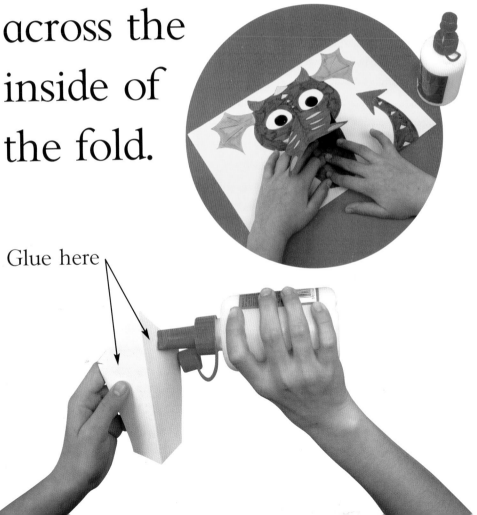

Glue here

Now, close up the card firmly and leave the glue to dry.

Opening up the card

Open up
the card.

The dragon's snout
moves, too.

Adding the tongue

Cut out a forked tongue.

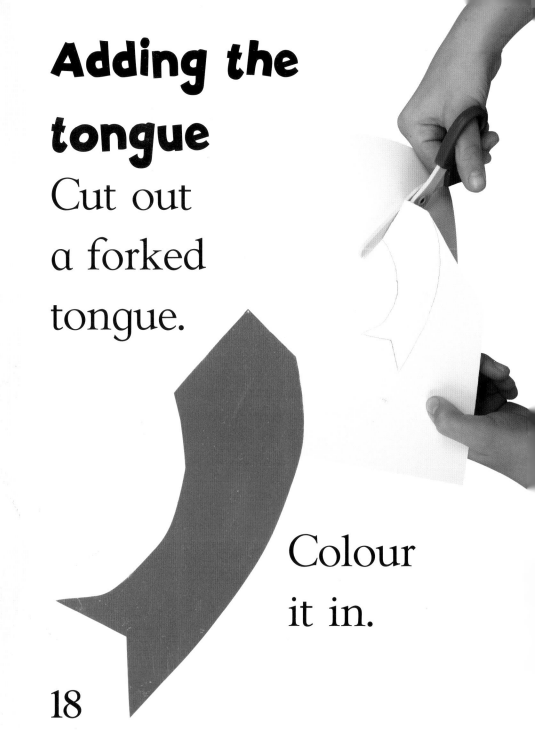

Colour it in.

Glue the tongue into
the dragon's mouth.

Finishing the card

Now decorate the front of the card.

You could draw a
hidden dragon.

Sending your card

Finally, you can write
in your card
and send it
to a friend.

23

Steps

Can you remember all of the steps to make your card?

1. Make the snout.

2. Colour in the snout.

3. Fold the card.

4. Draw the dragon.

5. Colour in the dragon.

6. Glue on the snout.

7. Glue on the tongue.

8. Colour in the front of the card.

9. Send your card to a friend.